I AM READY TO COME RIGHT AWAY

SHERAN ZELLOUS WHITE

D1452422

urbanpress

ISBN 978-1-63360-080-5
For Worldwide Distribution
Printed in the U.S.A.

Urban Press
P.O. Box 8881
Pittsburgh, PA 15221-0881
412.646.2780
www.urbanpress.us

FOREWORD

Many books have been written where the main character faces dire circumstances but escapes at the last moment. Tension builds until there is no way out, then someone or a fortuitous event rescues the heroine. In the real world we live in, however, rarely does such a last-minute rescue occur. Instead, we encounter difficult situations beyond our control that have dire consequences that can lead to loss, grief, and depression.

Sheran Zellous White is a dear friend of mine who has had several lifetimes of these serious circumstances (five in ten years), none with a storybook ending. Yet she is victorious and an overcomer, and buoyed by her faith in Jesus Christ, she reaches out to help the wounded and the marginalized. After the fifth death, God challenged her to share her experiences with you. This book is not a novel; it is the story of a loving woman pouring out her heart to help when you go through your own difficult situations.

Sheran has written "first person personal," sharing emotions as they well up within her from one or more of the traumas. Since emotions do not necessarily occur in the sequence in which the deaths occurred, I offer for clarity the following timeline of her losses:

- March 5, 2007; William James White, III, her 29-year-old son, was killed by gunshot.
- October 6, 2008; William James White, IV and Jordan James White, her 10- and four-year-old grandsons (sons of William James White, III) died in a house fire.
- October 8, 2009; William James White, Jr., her 54-year-old husband, died from a sudden heart attack.
- March 21, 2017; Devon Rae Marshman, her 22-year-old grandson, died in the infirmary of the State Correctional Institute-Pittsburgh from stage-four Hodgkin's lymphoma.

It is amazing and inspiring to see how Sheran's faith in Christ has given her such strength and assurance. She shares her story so you too can experience the same power and healing she has found.

G. Keith Turnbull
Chairman, Operations Board
Allegheny Center Alliance Church
Retired Executive Vice President for Strategic
    Analysis, Alcoa Corporation

INTRODUCTION

People who know the story of my life over the last decade have told me that I needed to write a book. I would think and pray about it, but I never sensed a release to do so. I never wanted to make the pain and suffering caused by the death of my family members to be the focus of my book. Every now and then, I would get a spark of inspiration to write a page or two on my own, but then I would shut down. As soon as my grandson passed into the presence of the Lord, I realized a book should not be about my journey, but rather about his testimony that describes where he has been, how he ended up there, where he is now, and how he got there as well. Even though his story is sad to some degree, it's also a miraculous story.

Finally, I feel our Lord has given me permission to tell of His goodness, faithfulness, mercy, and grace when the enemy tried to convince me He wasn't any of those things. Scripture tells us that the enemy comes to kill, steal, and destroy (see John 10:10). It doesn't say he will destroy but that he can steal. He works to convince us that he has that much power over us. Understanding that, I found the motivation and reason I needed to write – to help you understand that God can restore and heal whatever damage the enemy of our souls inflicts upon us.

Some people skip the foreword in books, but I always read them, because they usually describe the purpose the author had in mind when he or she wrote it. Therefore, let me tell you my purpose in this Introduction. I am writing to tell the story of a courageous young man, my grandson, Devon Rae Marshman. I hope that his story will help cause a movement for change, or at least a greater awareness concerning our prison and justice systems.

My grandson left a legacy with those who knew him, for he was a well-known, happy kid. When we visited him in the infirmary at the State Correction Institution-Pittsburgh, many of the medical staff would say how much they loved him, and his fellow patients would say the same. His fellow inmates would go out of their way to ask if we wanted water or if there was anything they could do to make us comfortable. I still pray for those inmates and all the other inmates and guards in that awful place.

The only reason we were permitted to visit was because my grandson's death was imminent. Otherwise, visitors in the infirmary were not allowed. The guards told us they had never seen anyone granted the privileges to come to the infirmary and walk through the prison as often as we did. The guard at the check point would ask, "Weren't you just here?" I would reply we were, and he would say he didn't know who we knew because no civilians had ever been allowed to go beyond where he regularly sat. I always told him I knew Jesus, to which he did not reply.

It was a real trek to get to the infirmary. We first went up an elevator and then all around through this door and that, and in the process, we got to see the inner workings of the prison, including the command center. At the time, what I saw did not impact me but since then I have had time to reflect on what we saw. That prison was shut down permanently on June 30. 2017 because of its age, run-down condition, and for political reasons unclear even to some of the staff and guards.

When I talked with the head nurse and one of the guards, they said they didn't know what they were going to do with the staff. All the guards and medical staff seemed upset that the facility was being shut down. Many of them would be transferred to other facilities as far as an hour away. From what I saw and knew, it was a facility that housed nonviolent offenders who all appeared to be under the age of 30. There were a couple of men in their 50s or 60s, but they wouldn't be sent there unless their crimes were nonviolent and stemmed from drugs, alcohol, or some other type of substance abuse. My grandson's offense wasn't any of those, but he was transferred there because of the medical care he needed that was only provided in Pittsburgh.

The shutdown included the hospital where my grandson was treated in his last days. It was a state-of-the-art infirmary, built specifically to care for inmates. The infirmary had a cancer center where they got their chemo, and doctors from various hospitals would come in to deliver care. When that facility closed, it took with it the only such infirmary for inmates in the Commonwealth of Pennsylvania, and it saddened me when I realized how important that infirmary was in my grandson's medical care during his last days on this side of life along with many other inmates who required serious medical attention. I don't know where they are treated now.

In the pages that follow, I want to tell you the life story of my grandson. It will include his early years when he lived with his grandfather and me. I will tell you what he did to receive the sentence that he did, and share why I feel the sentence was unjust. This won't be a book, however, complaining about racism or inequalities in the justice system, but a book of how God used my grandson's imprisonment for His purpose. It will be a sad but also a feel-good story of the reality of Romans 8:28: "For we know that God causes all things to work for good for those love God and are called according to His purpose."

I have chosen the title, *I Am Ready to Come Right Away,* because it is a phrase from a letter Devon's chaplain sent me after his death. I include that letter in its entirety later in this book, but I include an excerpt here so you understand why the title is so special to me:

> I found a request from him [Devon] asking to be added to the service list at a time when he was well enough to go. It was, of course, polite and respectful and included the words please and thank you. More importantly to me, however, was that his request ended with the sentence, "I am ready to come right away." Devon followed the command of our Lord and kept his lamp burning and his heart ready for service. So I take comfort in knowing that earlier this week, as the Lord came to put an end to Devon's struggle and suffering, Devon was able to answer our Savior with those same words—I am ready to come right away.

The chaplain did not have to send that letter, but it speaks to me of how many lives my grandson touched, even though he was at a place we would not have chosen him to be.

My grandson lived only 22 short years, but he touched many lives, perhaps more in death than in life. I want this book to honor his memory and to serve as a record for his surviving family, his mother, and his brothers. We have a responsibility to preserve his memory and build on his faith as a family. I also write to remind you, the reader, that not all young men who go to prison are bad boys or hoodlums, but have families and may have been treated unfairly by our overloaded legal system that sometimes makes mistakes. Most of all, however, I want to testify to God's goodness and love that have preserved me and my family not just to survive, but to live with joy in the midst of our pain. Join me now as I share the rest of the story about my grandson, Devon Rae Marshman—*I Am Ready to Come Right Away!*

Sheran Zellous White
Pittsburgh, PA
April 2018

Chapter One

THIS ONE WAS DIFFERENT

When my grandson entered the penal system, we expected him to serve the minimum time of his sentence as we continued to work to have his sentence reduced. We never expected his journey there to end after four years with his death. It saddened me that he never had a chance to come home and rebuild his life. He never had a chance to have a girlfriend, but thank God he never had any children to leave behind who would never have a relationship with their father, having to know him through the memories of others. His life truly was a different journey. I actually got to witness his passing, counting his last five breaths and watching his nostrils move ever so slightly while he was looking at me on Tuesday, March 21, 2017 at 1:15 PM. He died at the tender age of 22.

My husband died in 2009, and I don't think I ever grieved his passing. I didn't have time to do that because of my son's murder two years earlier in 2007 and the death of my son's two boys in a house fire in 2008. After those two tragedies, I believe my husband died of a broken heart exactly one year and two days after our grandsons died in that fire. In the aftermath of those losses, I had to minister to my daughter, the four living grandchildren, and my daughter-in-law, while trying to hold together what was left of my family.

The situation with my grandson happened quickly, and we really didn't think he would go to prison, especially for so long, for something relatively insignificant when compared to other crimes. He did go to prison and he died while serving his sentence, and I find myself in deep grief again. It's painful, but it's a different pain this time because I watched the whole process and saw it coming while with the others I was totally unprepared.

I didn't witness my son's shooting or see him lying in the street with snow on top of his body as he bled and died. I do remember standing close by and thinking that he had to be cold, because I thought he was still alive. The police wouldn't let us see him, and all I kept thinking was that it was snowing and I hoped they covered him up to keep him warm, but again I didn't get to see him.

I had my grandsons in church the Sunday before they died because I always had them in church. After church, I took them to the laundromat to wash some big blankets. There was a Steelers game in the evening, and I thought I needed to get them home to watch it. I had my daughter's three boys at the time because she was in the hospital recovering from a serious surgery, and my son's two boys were with us – all five grandsons.

I remember them running around the laundromat. The older of my son's two sons (who died in the fire) was 10 years old at the time, and he was chasing the other boys with a whiffle bat around the laundromat. He stopped and said to me, "You know what, Grandma? You need to beat these boys! They're out of control!" I laughed and just let them run around. Then I took the two grandsons home (the ten- and four-year-old), and they turned around and said goodbye and told me they loved me. At 1:16 AM, I got a phone call from their neighbor who lived across the street, asking if I was Aisha White's mother. When I responded that I was her mother-in-law, the caller informed me that Aisha's house was on fire. I got my daughter's three children out of bed right away and we drove the few blocks to their house.

My husband and I were separated for a while at that point because we were a textbook case of a marriage gone bad after the death of our adult child. Before we left the house the night of the fire, I hesitated calling him to tell him, but I made the call and he was there just seconds after we arrived. I thank God I made that call and he didn't hear about the fire on the news.

When my husband died, he was living in his own apartment. It was exactly one year and two days after the fire when my daughter-in-law came to my house asking where I had been because they had been calling me for hours. I didn't realize that I had left my cell phone in the car. She informed me that Mr. Bill, as she called my husband, had suffered a heart attack, so we went over to his apartment right away. Once there, I refused to go in and see him.

Now let's fast forward eight years, and I am holding

my grandson in the prison infirmary as he took his last breath. That was different, oh so different. With the others, I had no choice; I had to let them go. With my grandson, Devon, I didn't want to let him go, but I had a choice and chose to release him. He died in prison and we had to fight for every visit that we made to see him. It was always painful to have to leave him because he was so sick. I would promise that we would be back the next day, but I knew we would have to fight the bureaucracy to make it happen, and sometimes I could not keep my promise.

To visit him, we had to make phone calls to the head nurse, who wouldn't always return our calls. He wasn't their only patient, but he was my grandchild and he was my only patient. It had been difficult leaving him when we visited him in the normal visiting area when he was healthy. We would hear the guards say, "Marshman, it's time." I would hug and kiss him and wait for the guard to come get him along with all the other inmates who had visitors, while we went home to eat a meal far better than he and the others would receive. It was even more difficult to leave him when he was at his sickest and could barely sit up and carry on a conversation.

His voice was raspy and weak when he called or when he talked during our visits, so much so that we could barely understand what he was saying. To have to leave him like that was just horrible. All the while, however, God was gracious and merciful to the end, because the nurse had warned us that he would probably pass away quickly. She called one morning at 7:30 AM and told us to get there quickly. We were there within 10 minutes at most. He could have died in his sleep, in his cell and alone, but God gave us four hours to talk to, soothe, and comfort him. It wasn't disgusting. I had witnessed two cancer patients some years earlier as they received their Last Rites in a regular hospice setting. They weren't family members, but I remember how horrible their passing was. I will also never forget how offensive and toxic their breath was.

With my grandson, however, it was different. My daughter and I said we wished we could get that smell back because his breath smelled so sweet. While in the infirmary during those last hours of his life, I had him in my arms and couldn't hold him long enough. After that, his scent was all over my body. It was a strange smell while he was breathing, and his breath permeated the whole room, but it wasn't offensive. It wasn't like he was fighting for air. He was just breathing, and it got more and more shallow. Then it was over, and we were left once again to pick up the pieces of our lives that had been shattered by the passing of one more loved one.

I will never forget how beautiful Devon's parting was. It was like a television death that I watched but did not agonize over. Devon wasn't fighting to stay here. He was listening to me and my daughter's voice. I was massaging his scalp and he was at peace. At one point, he stopped breathing. His eyes were open, and it looked like he was daydreaming until the nurse came in and closed his eyes. It was amazing.

As painful as this was and is, however, it was indeed a different kind of pain than I had experienced in the loss of the others described in this chapter. Let's move on so you can find out more about what my grandson did that put in motion the end of his life I have just described.

Chapter Two
IN PRISON

Devon had just turned 18 in August of 2012 and was sentenced in September of 2013. He received a sentence to serve prison time for between four to eight years and was sent to a prison in Houtzdale, PA. He was charged with robbery of a vehicle, possession of stolen property, false identification, and eluding and evading arrest. Devon was driving a car when the police pulled up behind him. He and three passengers jumped out of the car and ran. The other young men were only 17 and were released without charges. The car he was driving had been stolen (Devon did not steal it) from a pizza delivery man who had also been robbed and the authorities wanted Devon to divulge who he "rented" the car from. When he would not tell them, I believe that is why they gave him a harsh sentence. We will talk about his trial and sentence in Chapter Six.

After sentencing, Devon went back to the county jail and we were not allowed to see him. By the time he got the paperwork for us to go see him, they were moving him to Camp Hill, where all the inmates are processed. Devon wrote me a letter from there, which I found while I was looking for another document. It was his first letter, and I initially read it when I was having a really bad day. It said, "The psych doctor told me they don't give out injections, but down in the county they did. So right now, they are giving me pills to keep me stable. I just wanted to tell you I love you, I'm okay, I'm doing fine, and I will see you soon."

Before he committed the crime, Devon was experiencing behavior changes and was starting to act out, and we couldn't understand why. Then my daughter took him to a program called JRS and they diagnosed him with schizophrenia. Once they put him on the medication, he was fine. While he was waiting to go to trial, he was fine. He was medicated while he was on trial, and my concern was that he would not get his proper medications in prison. When he didn't, he would start to hear voices.

When he got into the county jail, I called the ADA, who was always very kind to me. I said I needed to know how I could be sure he gets his medication. He said he'd make a phone call, and Devon never missed getting any from that time forward. Then he went to Camp Hill and never missed it there. He said down at County they were giving injections, rather than the pills. When he got to Camp Hill, they didn't give injections. Instead they gave him pills, and he said he was getting them and was fine.

He was at Camp Hill for about six months and then he was sent to his home prison, as they call it, in SCI-Houtzdale, which is an hour outside of Johnstown. He was there for about six months before he was allowed visitors. To be approved as a visitor, we had to provide pictures and all kinds of personal information so they could check to make sure we didn't have a prison record.

Even though we didn't see him for a year, we were not anxious because his letters were upbeat, and he was getting his meds. He got a radio and was enjoying his music. My daughter kept all the letters I sent him. There was one letter about him responding to the radio that only got one Christian station, and the song he was describing. There is also an email system in place, so we could send him email after we got him an iPad and I could write back to him. When we started visiting, we had abandoned any hope of a new trial or reduced sentence.

His prison destination at Houtzdale was nice as far as prisons go. We all thought he would serve his four years at Houtzdale, but that all changed so quickly. They had a lot of programs for the inmates. Devon was enrolled in art classes there because he was a gifted artist and could draw and sketch anybody. The prison also had a school system come in and prepare the inmates for their GED exam, and Devon took those classes and earned his GED diploma. He was a good kid and wasn't stupid, but he did make a serious mistake.

We would not visit him at Houtzdale very often because it was a two-and-a-half hour drive, and during winter months, it was difficult getting there. My daughter and I went together, and his brothers went up to see him twice. When his brothers visited him, he would always warn them not to do anything that would cause them to do prison time. He didn't say it every time they visited, and he would say it casually, but he said it enough for them to get the picture. All the time we were there, and in his letters, Devon would complain that he had serious back pain. He was a tall kid, and he said his feet were hanging over the end of the bed. We thought the pain was caused by the short bed or the thin mattress.

It was a source of frustration and concern that he could not get any relief. When he went to the infirmary, they would give him Ibuprofen or some other painkiller, and that went on for two years. One time when he presented himself to the infirmary, however, he collapsed. Two days later, he was taken to Altoona Hospital and then transferred to Shadyside Hillman Cancer Center. The Hillman Center called his mother to inform her that he was in imminent danger. They told her that he felt clammy to the touch, was in severe pain, and in a weakened condition, but until death was imminent, we could not see him.

My daughter and I made phone calls to people who had compassion on us and we were granted permission to see him, but only once at Shadyside Hillman. It was gut-wrenching to go there and see him shackled to the bed with armed guards in the room, as if he was a dangerous drug lord like El Chapo. Devon was a non-violent, critically-ill young man needing comfort and desiring to see his mom and grandmother. I promised earlier that I would not turn this book into an indictment against the penal system, but that was ridiculous in my opinion. While he was there at Hillman, he was diagnosed with stage four Hodgkin's lymphoma.

Back at Houtzdale, his home prison, they had a nice graduation ceremony for the students, but he had collapsed by then and had been brought back to Pittsburgh, thus missing his graduation. The officials hoped he could come back to Houtzdale because he was the class valedictorian and they were quite impressed with him. They had the GED graduation without him, however, and they mailed him his diploma. He spent two years on the North Side of Pittsburgh getting his cancer treatments once he was transferred to State Correctional Institution - Pittsburgh (SCIP). He had been receiving them at an outside hospital for a while, but once they got him stabilized, he was treated in the prison infirmary like everyone else.

He was receiving chemotherapy and, from what I understood, he also had some surgeries. We don't know what the surgeries were because the officials were not required to let us know. To this day, we don't know what his medical care was outside of the chemo and he didn't know either so he could not inform us. He was confused and so young to be facing that alone. He didn't understand the diagnosis, and certainly didn't look like a typical cancer patient. He had beautiful hair which he cut off because he thought he would lose it. He never went bald, however, and it just grew back, even after his chemo.

The next time we could see him was when death was imminent at West Penn Hospital in Pittsburgh. This was the last time he was transferred from the prison to AGH and died just weeks afterwards. An oncologist came in and reported that they were first going to put a stint in to repair the hole in Devon's esophagus before they could proceed with any other procedures involving the treatment of the Hodgkin's. Devon had told me on the phone earlier that it felt as though his food would drop right down into his belly when he ate. They tried to fix that hole but it didn't work, so the doctor wanted to try and repair it again. After that, he would start the chemo treatments, and later administer radiation. That would be followed by a bone marrow transplant. At that point, Devon asked how long he had to live. The oncologist said with treatment he could live six months to two years but without treatment, he would only live six more months at the most. When Devon heard that, he looked at the oncologist and said, "I'm stopping all treatment."

When the doctor heard that, he became irate. The doctor explained again what they were going to do, knowing it was only to prolong the inevitable. Once again, my grandson insisted that all treatment be stopped. The doctor warned him again that if he stopped, he would only live for six months, but with treatment, six months to two years. My grandson looked at me and said, "I have made my decision."

He expected me to react and try to convince him to change his mind. At first, I looked at him (as only a mother or grandmother can do) but he turned his head away from me. Then I demanded, "Look at me." He turned to look at me and I said, "I'm not angry with you." After that, he changed the subject and asked, "How's Aunt Venita?" The doctor departed and that was it. His mother was sitting there with me and we talked. He wanted to know how everyone was doing and went down the list, asking who's doing this, that, and the other. Then he got sleepy and we let him go to sleep since it was about 10:00 PM. I promised we would see him the next day, but he responded, "No you won't." He said they would take him back to the prison, and that's exactly what they did. He lived for two weeks after that.

When he got back to the Northside prison, they put him in the infirmary where he became quite upset. He didn't want to be in the infirmary, but preferred to be on the cell block with his friends. He wanted to feel like he was living his last days as a normal person, so they put him back. That didn't last long, however, for the guards were concerned because he was having difficulty breathing. He had a cell by himself in which he was walking around, as weak as he was, and would "kick it with the homies," as he would say. The guards feared that he could collapse and "code" on them, or cause any number of medical emergencies that they were not equipped to handle as non-medical personnel. They also felt too much of their time was spent watching him and not the rest of the men on the block. It wasn't safe for anyone and they insisted he go back to the infirmary for his and others' safety.

He was not happy having to be go back to infirmary without his friends. The infirmary was much nicer and cleaner, and there he had his own bathroom with a tub. He could take hot baths daily, expressing his appreciation more than once for that bit of privacy and comfort. He had a standard hospital bed with a full mattress, unlike the cell beds, which he described as a wire base with a very thin mattress. He also had a flat-screen television mounted on the wall. He was cold all the time, so the head nurse gave him a space heater that he kept close to his bed and I was concerned he would burn himself. I later discovered the command center could see his every move, along with ours when we visited. That gave me a little peace about the space heater.

As I already stated, it was difficult to visit him at the prison. On one occasion after his release from AGH and return to the infirmary for the beginning of comfort measures, they told us we could visit when he was in the infirmary, promising to bring him down to us (we weren't permitted in the infirmary at that point). We came in and went through all the regular visitor checkpoints. Once we were seated and awaiting his arrival to the visitor area, a guard who checked in visitors entered the visitor area and in front of everyone started yelling, "I'm sorry, but your grandson is not going to be able to come down here! He's doing real bad!" I immediately start crying, and my oldest grandson Jerome, who is a large man, was livid and said, "You came in here and made my grandmother cry." The guard responded, "Well, I, I'm just saying he can't come, so you have to go." And that was that.

We were in the visiting area and everyone was glaring at us, some with obvious compassion. I put my coat over my head because I couldn't control my tears. I was scared to death, fearing he had taken a turn for the worse, and the guard's panicked screaming didn't make matters any better. When we got home, Devon called to say he thought we were coming to see him. When I told him we were there, he asked when and I told him that we just had gotten back home. He said they hadn't told him we were there and then he started yelling for the CO while I was still on the phone, asking why they didn't tell him his family was there. I warned him not to act out, but he had an intense conversation with someone and from that point on, we were able to see him – not down in the visitor's area, but in the infirmary. The Lord worked it out for us that we were able to see him so often during his last weeks on earth.

Chapter Three
"SAVED!"

There was a dramatic change the last few times we saw him. He looked and acted more like a man and was no longer that boy he was when he went in. I wondered how he would do because you hear horror stories about life inside prison. He was serving his time effortlessly, with no complaints or concerns. There were no signs of fear and he never felt threatened. I even received a letter from the Assistant District Attorney after Devon passed, saying he remembered how Devon handled a difficult case with dignity. The ADA saw his maturity before I did. I credit this to the Lord's intervention and intercession.

April 17, 2017

Dear Ms. White,

I received a copy of your letter to Judge Philip Ignelzi and I am very sorry to hear of the passing of your grandson, Devon Marshman. Though I had very little contact with the young man, it was my impression of Mr. Marshman that he handled the difficult process of the criminal case against him in an upright and dignified manner. I was equally impressed with the members of his family, including you, as I recall, who attended his court dates and later notified me of his illness. Your concern and love for him was obvious. I have no doubt that it was a great comfort to Mr. Marshman that both you and his mother were by his side as he passed on. I am certain from the tone of your letter that you share my own belief that Devon has passed on to a greater peace and contentment with the Lord than any of us can experience in this life.

Regarding Mr. Marshman's criminal history, Title 18 Section 9122 (b) of the Pennsylvania Crimes Code governing expungement provides that a criminal history record may be expunged when a person who is the subject of the criminal information (the charging document) has been dead for three years.

Accordingly, this provision would apply to Mr. Marshman's case in late March of 2020, and you could seek an expungement of his record at that time.

Again, I am very sorry for your loss. Please do not hesitate to contact me if you have any further questions.

Truly Yours,

Chris Stone
Assistant District Attorney

Devon never said things to us like "get me out of here." Instead, he would apologize and say, "I'm sorry, Grandma, that I put you through all this. I made a mistake." I always told him that we were not going to keep looking back, but were looking forward. I would tell him how proud I was of him and that I loved him. He never gave any indication that it was hard for him, until the last few weeks when he got sick. Then he wanted badly to come home to see his brothers, who he had not seen in weeks. He talked to them on the phone, but his voice got so weak that we could barely hear him.

During his last days, he knew we were working on him being released. We got an attorney, and the parole board came to see him to make arrangements, questioning him about a home plan. That allowed him to rest comfortably the last couple of weeks, knowing we were working on that and the parole board was cooperating.

We never got him out, but God got him out in a way I never anticipated. I rested in the fact that it was better the Lord's way than our way. I'm so thankful that the Lord always goes before us. At the time, we were unable to handle that difficult situation. We would have been trying to care for Devon in his fragile condition, but God knew our hearts and Devon's desire to be set free and the Lord did just that – set him free. I often tell people that our Lord promises to heal us, and that healing can be either on this side of life or in His presence. His Word tells us in John 14:3, "And if I go and prepare a place for you, I will come back and take you to be with me that you also may be where I am." Thank You, Jesus.

His funeral was beautiful. Pastor Blaine Workman, one of my church's pastors, did a wonderful job. We were at the funeral home during the visitation and Pastor Blaine came in and got a feel for how we wanted things to go, and asked if we wanted anyone to come up and say a few words, and we said absolutely not, not even his brother Jerome. I didn't want anyone getting up there to distract from the primary purpose of the service, which was to share the love of God and celebrate His mercy and grace to us before, during, and after Devon got sick. We also wanted to celebrate Devon's short life that he lived with much purpose, even in the dark places where he found himself.

Nate Boersma, an opera singer from the worship team at my church, sang two songs that Devon really liked. The night we were at West Penn Hospital when he made his decision to stop all treatment, Devon asked out of the blue if I had heard of a group called Casting Crowns. Of course I had, and he informed me that he liked them, especially a song they sing called *Good, Good Father*. In one of his first letters I received from him when he was in SCI-Houtzdale, he wrote out the words from another contemporary worship song, *Indescribable*. He thought the song said, "indescribable, uncontainable, you placed the stars in the sky and *you know my name*." The song actual says "and you know them by name" I believe God let him hear His heart for him because the Lord did indeed know him by name.

Early in his sentence, I don't think he was in SCI-Houtzdale for only a month when he asked for $30 to buy a radio for his cell. He went to the commissary where he and the other inmates purchase personal items like candy, bought a radio, and then wrote me a letter telling me that the radio only got one station, but it was a Christian station. That's when he first heard Indescribable. We had done what we could for him while he was serving his sentence, but I wish we could have done more.

During the funeral, Pastor Blaine told a story I had shared with him that happened when Devon was probably nine and Jerome was eleven. When they came home after going to church with my mother-in-law, my husband was downstairs watching football on television and I was upstairs reading the Bible. I heard the screen door slam and someone came running up the steps, tripping as he ran. Devon threw open the door and said to me, "Guess what? Me and Jerome got, we got, we got, umm, what is it Jerome?" And Jerome said, "Saved." My grandson said, "Yeah, that's it. We got *saaaaaaved*. I have Jesus in my heart!"

I was beside myself with joy, jumping up and down and screaming. My husband asked what was going on, and I came down to tell him that the boys had been saved today. We were all excited and Devon was absolutely elated. The following August, I decided to get baptized, and Jerome asked to get baptized with me. Then Devon said he wanted to be baptized as well. We all went through the classes to prepare and got baptized at Turnbull Lake in 2002.

Prior to the baptism, the boys had always been in church with me along with my other grandchildren; but once they were baptized, church meant much more to them. My son and his wife appreciated them going

because it gave them three or four hours they could spend together while their three children went to church with me. We would have dinner at my house and then I'd take them home. That went on for years. All six of my grandchildren were raised and nurtured in their faith at Allegheny Center Alliance Church.

I took a picture of Devon's name from the kiosk at the funeral home and posted it on Facebook. Someone wrote in a post that she had never experienced such a wonderful homegoing service in her entire life. It was truly a celebration and was absolutely beautiful. After

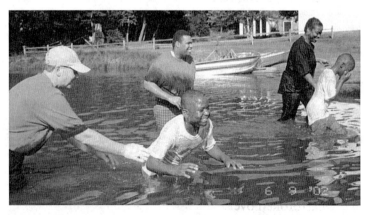

Pastor Blaine told the story about my grandsons getting "saved," intermittently during the service, he would say during the sermon, "What's that word again? What's that word again?" And everyone would say, "Saaaaaved."

During the funeral, I was at peace. I shed one tear when Nate was singing, only because he sang so beautifully. It was not a tear over concern where my grandson was or that he had departed this life. At that moment, the past and the present weren't there. His future in the presence of our Lord was what I was seeing and feeling. Nate's singing was only a confirmation I was hearing from our Lord. It was truly a celebration. There was no question as to where my grandson was. Not only was the service beautiful, but the day was also, the temperature being 50 degrees on March 25.

I remember going to the infirmary before he died with my coat on because it was so bitterly cold. During the funeral on March 25, rain was predicted, but it didn't come. I hosted a meal after the service at my house, because I prefer the intimacy of family and very close friends in the comfort of my home. It's my way of expressing my love language, and that's how my family has always done it. I had thirty to forty guests at my house, inside and outside. There was not much crying but a whole lot of laughter.

My son's daughter, Devon's cousin, and my daughter-in-law survived the house fire that took the lives of the two boys, and we didn't allow my granddaughter to go my husband's funeral or her brothers' funeral. She does remember her father's (my son's) funeral. On the day of Devon's funeral, I believe she was finally grieving all her losses. They were less like cousins and raised with her like brothers and sister, and she wept. I tried to console her as I held her because her mother was unable to do so. She was heartbroken over the loss of Devon, but everyone else was able to keep their composure as much as they could. It is partly due to the way Pastor Blaine conducted the service. He made it a time to remember who the primary focus was, and that focus was Jesus, inviting those present to make a commitment to Christ so they too would be in paradise one day with Devon. As always, the real work of mourning begins after the funeral is over. This was the case with Devon as well.

Chapter Four
AFTER THE FUNERAL

After the funeral, the grieving started for me when I thought of all the "what ifs" for Devon's life. We had hoped he would be out in time for his brother's high school graduation. We were planning to celebrate his graduation accomplishment from Houtzdale at the same time. We had secured the services of a law firm to begin the proceedings for a compassion release. The prison system had a protocol in place so that when an inmate was determined to be near death, the inmate would be granted a compassion release. The prison began those proceedings even before our intervention. When Devon could barely be heard on the phone, he called to inform us that someone from the parole board had been there to see him two days in a row. If nothing else, he passed knowing he was going to be released.

Now I mourn the lost opportunities for his life, what could have been, should have been. It's especially tough for my daughter, his mother, who is going through a tough time as any mother would. I know what she is going through. Unfortunately, I too have experienced the loss of child, my son and her brother ten years earlier, almost to the exact date.

I get calls and texts from her, and it's difficult to minister to her, but God always gives me strength to do so. At the same time, I'm tired, both emotionally and physically. The months after Devon's passing were a real challenge. The funeral still serves as a source of true comfort for me. I wish it had been recorded, for it truly celebrated Devon's life and the legacy he left in his short time on earth. I am including the letter that the chaplain wrote as a tribute to Devon, and I was surprised and delighted to see her attend the funeral, which she did not have to do.

To the family of Devon Marshman,

I'm thankful to have the opportunity to offer my condolences for your loss. I am aware that it is a significant loss, not only because of Devon's age, but because of the person that he was. People sometimes think that men within the institution can be lumped in a group and assigned a label. But the truth is, the institution is a community unto itself and Devon was well thought of within his community at SCI-Pittsburgh, where he was recognized as a special person. During his time with us, he impacted both staff and his peers with his upbeat, caring, and respectful attitude. People in the institution describe him as helpful, thoughtful, and polite. But it's the other men's treatment of him that truly gives the picture of how much he was liked. In a Bible study I held on his unit, when asked for prayer requests, men often asked for prayer for him. When he was ill, other men who lived on his unit volunteered to help with him. Because he was so kind with others, people responded by wanting to be kind to him. In the Gospel of Matthew (5:16), Jesus tells us that we are to let our light shine before men. Sometimes, he asks us to do that in dark and difficult places. That's what Devon did in our institution. And many were grateful for his light. In the Gospel of Luke (12:35), Jesus says, "Be dressed, ready for service and keep your lamps burning." I looked into Devon's chapel file. At our institution, men need to request to get a pass to come to religious services. Although Devon couldn't always come because he was often in the infirmary, I found a request for him asking to be added to the service list at a time when he was well enough to go. It was, of course, polite and respectful and included the words please and thank you. More importantly to me, however, his request ended with this sentence: "I am ready to come right away." Devon followed the command of our Lord and kept his lamp burning and his heart ready for servivce. So I take comfort in knowing that earlier this week, as the Lord came to put an end to Devon's struggle and suffering, Devon was able to answer our Savior with those same words—I am ready to come right away. Thanks be to our gracious God. He has gone home to a place where illness and even death have no power over him anymore. And while those of us who were blessed to know him will miss him, we have the sure and certain promise that we will see him again, healed, whole and still oh so special when we meet in God's kingdom.

*With my sympathies and
prayers for your comfort,*

*Rev. Tami Hooker
Facility Chaplaincy Program Director*

When I contrast that funeral with the one for my grandsons who died in the fire, there is no comparison. That was an extremely difficult time when we had to bury two small bodies. It had only been seventeen months after we had buried their father, my son. It is painful to remember their funeral and that is my daughter-in-law's testimony so I will only touch on my own emotions at that time. However, I know where they are too.

My son's funeral was overwhelming. There were so many people at his funeral. One of my good friends said she waited in line for thirty minutes and thought the whole state of Pennsylvania was there. It was unbelievable the number of people who showed up for the visitation, but that was my son. Everything he did was over the top, so of course his homegoing was over the top as well.

I don't remember much of my husband's funeral. I have a memory of the visitation at Coston Funeral Home on the Northside. When my husband, who was more like Devon's dad, died of a heart attack, Devon was the one I had to console in the sanctuary, because he was standing at the casket crying and acting out. He wasn't acting out in the sense that it was audible. He was throwing his arms up in the air, not knowing what to do, crying and walking in a circle. I had to get up, hug and kiss him, and gently bring him to sit next to me. He just laid in my arms during the funeral service, crying the whole time. We had shared many such intimate moments together with him in my arms and me consoling him.

That's about as much as I can remember of my husband's funeral. I'm almost certain Pastor Rock officiated it, and I specifically asked Pastor Blaine to do Devon's, because from the time Devon was arrested, Pastor Blaine was the person I would share and keep up to date over those four years.

Often God will give glimmers of things to come. We don't always see them at that time. Looking back, I can clearly see God being where He always is – right there with me and them. His Word tells us in Isaiah 55:8, "'For My thoughts are not your thoughts, nor are your ways My ways,' declares the Lord." I recently heard Pastor Rick Warren say that we don't realize God is all we need when He is all we have. I have said that in a different way to many people. When they ask if I am angry with God, I immediately reply, "Absolutely not; how could I when He is all I got?" It's during these times of trials that one really gets to see Him at work in one's life. I don't blame God for any of this. This is a sinful world and most bad things happen because of the actions and choices of people. When they happen, our Lord is quick to step in and comfort, restore, refresh, and remind us where our help comes from; it comes from the Lord.

After many years of looking back, I can truly say that God is good and He only gives good gifts. Those gifts are not the kind we give to one another that wear out, burn up, or decay, or that we may like or dislike, accept or reject. His gifts are those promises of His goodness, faithfulness, love, grace, and mercy. Those gifts are eternal: "So we fix our eyes not on what is seen, but on what is unseen, since what is seen is temporary, but what is unseen is eternal" (2 Corinthians 4:18).

Speaking of looking back, it's time for me to explain why I was so close to Devon and all of my grandchildren. Let's go back to the beginning of their lives now.

Chapter Five

GROWING UP

There is a saying that goes like this: Your son is your son till he finds a wife; your daughter is your daughter all your life. Mothers seem to have a closer relationship with their daughter and their kids, perhaps because the daughter always tends to come back home. When my son married, he had his family and made time for them, so his children really seemed like my grandchildren. My daughter's children, Devon included, were more like my own kids because she would always leave them with us. She was a young mom but a good one.

My daughter was living with us at home when she had her first two children, so they spent most of their infant years with us. The youngest, however, did not live with us after he was born. He was, and still is, attached to his mother. They all are, but when the first two were born, we had them for a while. Thus, when all three came to live with us, it was quite difficult. The youngest was four or five and he wanted his mother. He would cry and there was no consoling him. When he would awaken, she wasn't there. For the other two, it was nothing, for our home was like their real home to them. It wasn't odd or an imposition for my husband and me because we had a close relationship with our kids and grandkids all their lives.

Devon and his brothers lived with my husband and me on and off for seven years. The reasons are part of my daughter's testimony and not mine, so I will allow her to tell that story when and how she chooses. She was facing some obstacles in her life at the time, and we all felt it was best for the boys to stay with us during those times. It was a joint decision and she was still involved in their lives. The boys were five, seven, and nine years old when they first came to live with us.

That was difficult for my husband and me. We were in our forties and our two children had been out of the house for a while. We had to cope with a five-year-old crying for his mother, and there was nothing we could do to console him. Obviously, they all spent a lot of time with us over those years, which is why we were so close to them all when Devon was sentenced and became sick. They were also close with my son, their uncle, since he was only a few years older than the oldest grandson. We became like parents to them rather than grandparents. We were the disciplinarians, making them do homework, taking them to school, picking them up, and signing them up for their sports activities. Devon played football in the West End. My husband enjoyed those years and worked with them like he was building a softball team, the sport he loved to play.

I have always worked outside the home, so I had to juggle work duties and being a surrogate mom. When they first came to live with us, I was working at Central Medical Center. Then I went to work at Gateway Health Plan. By the time I got here, she had taken the boys back full time and they were doing very well. My husband worked at the Central Blood Bank, then at Smith Klein Beecham, and at Quest Diagnostics. When he died, he was working at Allegheny General Hospital, serving as office manager for a nephrologist. We have always had jobs and were never without.

Our grandsons were latch-key kids, just like our children were. They had keys to our house when they came home from school, they were at home until we came home from work. We would get home, make dinner, and do whatever needed to be done to get ready for the next day.

School was at the bottom of the hill where we lived. Dale Harper, one of the men in our church, was their teacher. When Dale came to Devon's viewing, he said he remembered the two oldest boys, Jerome and Devon but not the youngest one, DeonDre. Dale said he remembered Devon was the one he always had to put his arm out to stop him because Devon was always running around, busy and into everything all the time. Jerome, the oldest, was the one who was reserved and quiet. Devon was quite active then and up until his passing

Devon was also quite humorous, but it didn't take much for him to cry. His nickname was "Pooder" because when as a small child he cried, he would hold his breath, then let it out all at once between his lips and make a "poooo" sound. When I heard that, I said he was such a little Pooder. That was his name on the streets among his friends and in our family. Hardly anyone called him Devon, except me. How ironic he would hold his breath as a small child but when he passed, his breathing was free, so soft and quiet. He was not struggling to stay here and he did not shed one tear.

Devon was a fantastic artist. Had he gone to art school, only God knows what he could have been. He drew a picture of my son from a photo taken at my son's wedding, which of course is special and hangs in a frame in my dining room. He was gifted and no one else in the family could draw like he could. He was never a bad kid. He just made a bad decision, when he chose to ride around in that stolen car.

They were all good athletes, especially the youngest of the three, DeonDre, but he didn't enjoy playing. Devon could take it or leave it, but the reason he played was to earn the team jacket. Devon was the one who struggled the most when my husband died. It just got to be too much with his uncle dying suddenly, and a year later the boys, his cousins, dying in a fire.

Church became a part of my life when I became a born-again Christian in the year 2000. It took me about a year to find a church, and I ended up at Allegheny Center Alliance Church (ACAC) at someone's suggestion. They said I would fit right in at the church, and they were right. That first Sunday I came to church, I sat way in the back wondering when the pastor was going to come out. The next thing I knew, church was over, and I said to myself, "The pastor is white!" I assumed this church was a black church since it was on the Northside. There were a lot of black people sitting in the sanctuary at that time, but I had no idea Pastor Rock was the pastor. I was sitting there waiting for the real pastor to show up while Pastor Rock was giving the sermon.

Once I realized this was going to be my church home, I had only four grandchildren at that time and they were in church every week with me. Three were my daughter's sons and the other was my son's son who later died in the fire. The four-year-old grandson who died in the fire and my only granddaughter were not born at that time. I picked them all up every Sunday and they loved it. They were all in the children's choir, and came to the church from the early 2000s until they were in middle and high school. Everyone seemed to remember Jerome and DeonDre, the oldest and the youngest. When I had asked for letters of support for Devon from student ministries and children's ministries, however, no one seemed to remember him. It was another challenge for me as we faced the dilemma of his imprisonment.

When children get older, they are often tested in their faith. And it is not as easy for them to avoid temptation and trouble. I had always warned my grandchildren never to do anything wrong, for they would always get caught. That was the case with Devon, as I will explain in the next chapter.

Chapter Six

THE CRIME

Devon never got into trouble, just that one time that led to his arrest. I always told them two things. I didn't want them bringing home any babies. The second was not to get caught up in the system. None of them had babies and none of them went to prison. But one night, Devon got in that car with three other boys. He was 18 and they were 17. They dismissed those other boys but retained him because he was driving. I always told him that if he did anything, he was going to get caught because he knew better, and he would always be the one who would get caught.

Devon was in his junior year of high school when

he was arrested. All my grandkids were held back the year my two grandsons, their cousins, died in the fire. That's why he was a year behind. Was he going to school like he should? No. Was he hanging out with his friends? Yes. I never really got the story straight, but apparently somebody carjacked a pizza man and was renting the car out to young boys. He somehow rented it and he was caught with it. When the officials discovered the car was stolen and involved in a car-jacking, they tried to finger him as the one who had done the carjacking. He was put in a lineup and the pizza delivery man positively said Devon was not the one.

The police, however, suspected Devon knew the man from whom he got the car. He didn't tell who he got the car from. He had to live with that, and he did. Even the prosecuting attorney attested to the fact that Devon took his harsh sentence like a man.

My daughter called me to let me know that Devon had been arrested, and said that we needed to get bail money together. I didn't know how to do it, having never faced that before. We had to go down to the bail bondsmen, because Devon was down in the county jail. It was a significant amount of money and I refused to put my house up as collateral, somehow managing to put together the cash for bail. (The way bail works is that if the person out on bail doesn't show up, the bail money is forfeited, every penny of it. The bail does allow them to be free until their trial, which can take up to three years to occur.)

It's an intimidating process to secure bail. The bail bondsmen wanted all my information, and they took my social security number and bank account information. They really pressed me to put my house up but I refused. I got the money and got him out. He was out for about a year before his case went to trial, because the trial kept getting postponed. I know now that we made a poor decision to have Devon represented by a public defender. We didn't think what he had done was that serious, for he had only been driving around in a stolen car. We were wrong.

Our public defender was horrible and Devon was given a sentence of four to eight years. After his sentencing, I approached the prosecutor. I told him that our attorney, and I said it loud enough so my attorney and judge could hear me, was horrible. I questioned if he even had a soul. Everyone in the courtroom was looking at me as if I had lost my mind, and in a sense, I had. My grandson had already been taken out of the court by then and I was beside myself with anger and grief.

I asked the prosecutor what I could do about this because the public defender was so incompetent and I wanted to file a complaint against him. The prosecutor said that he shouldn't even talk to me, but he told me I could call the public defender's office to file a complaint there.

The ongoing delays for the year leading up to the trial were horrendous. We were not running up a bill with our attorney, since he was a public defender, but it was frustrating because of the uncertainty of what was going to happen. We tried to live our lives like we normally did. Then we went to court and, just like that, our lives changed.

During our year-long wait, Devon was like a normal teenager with no idea what was going on and what he was up against. At the suggestion of the public defender, Devon waved his right to a jury trial, because the public defender secured for us a "plea bargain." Initially they wanted to give him 5-10 years and the plea bargain was 4-8. We sat in the courtroom for three or four trials before his, so I had a chance to watch the process and observe the judge.

It was a gut-wrenching experience as we sat there, because we didn't know what was going to happen. We were sitting there and watching the people being sentenced. No one was going home or being freed, and all were black. When I observed that, I started to get a bad feeling, but I tried to stay positive.

When our proceedings began, the prosecuting attorney stated the charges and said something about a gun but my grandson said he didn't have a gun. The judge looked at both the attorneys and called them to the bench. They both went up there, but no one was talking but the prosecuting attorney. Our attorney wasn't saying anything, but the judge dismissed the gun charge. Then the judge said there was a plea bargain and asked my grandson if he accepted the plea bargain. We didn't know what was going on, and the judge said the sentence would be four to eight years.

At this point, we knew things were more serious than we realized and that we had not been adequately prepared. My heart started to race when they took Devon away in handcuffs, and I was thinking, "Over a car, my God, over a car? Four to eight years? Nobody was hurt. Nobody was shot." It was incredibly sad.

I was thinking he would be placed under house arrest, or given significant community service duties. After all, he was only 18! That's what I wrote in a letter to the judge. I said I wanted to commend him on how he operated his courtroom after sitting and watching him work. He was attentive, keeping the attorneys on task, and he knew what was going on. My letter was not to complain about him but about the attorney I had, and how poorly we were represented. My taxpayer dollars were paying for someone who wasn't doing their job.

We felt marginalized by the way the public defender

handled the case. I heard from Mr. Dugan who said he was going to talk to our attorney about it and wanted me to be there. By that time, I was only trying to find out where my grandson was going. I don't think he ever got back to me, but in all the confusion and grief, maybe he did and I missed it – but I never found an email from him. Here is the letter I sent to the presiding judge.

October 10, 2013

Your Honor,

> *First, I would like to express my appreciation on how you conduct your courtroom. I have been in your presence three times and upon my observation you are always on time; you keep all the attorneys on task and you show compassion toward the victim and the defendant. You are fully engaged and make sure everyone has a clear understanding of their rights before you pass judgment or sentencing.*
>
> *My reason for writing this letter is to express my disappointment and what I know to be an injustice with the legal representation by Mr. X for my grandson, Devon Marshman before you on October 7, 2013. For example, because you were engaged in the details you recognized there was a problem when my grandson, Devon Marshman, stated "I did not have a gun." You called counsels to your desk for a conference. I suspected you saw a problem that he was pleading guilty to armed robbery but he clearly said he didn't have a gun. I noticed that the prosecuting attorney, Mr. Y, had*

comments but my grandson's attorney, Mr. X, said nothing. When counsel went back to their positions you asked Mr. Y if had anything further to say before you passed judgment; he said no. Then you asked Mr. X and he too said no. I felt that was his opportunity to inform you and the prosecutor that my grandson, Devon Marshman, had never committed a crime prior to this case; had been diagnosed with schizophrenia four months after the arrest; which was probably the reason for his change in behavior; that he is currently on medication; in a program with the Jewish Residential Services (JRS); living in a group home under supervision of two therapists; was crime free up to the date of the trial and he was really unsure of what was happening due to his mental condition. However, Mr. X stood there and shook his head and plainly said no. I was shocked and appalled. Before all this I noticed he had no file on Devon and when we asked him what was going to be his defense, he just shrugged his shoulders and shook his head. I knew we were in trouble at that point.

After you sentenced Devon, I was in tears and spoke to Mr. Y. He showed more compassion towards to me than Mr. X. I asked how I could make a complaint against Mr. X and he informed I could file a complaint with the Public Defender's office, of which, I have already done. Mr. Matt Dugan was quick to respond to my email and followed up with Mr. Y. Matt said that Mr. Y said the 4-8 years was the lowest he could go with the plea and that came *from his superior(s) not him and he felt he had a strong enough case to back that up. I understand the sentencing could have carried a much longer prison term with each charge carrying its own length of time and being served consecutively. Matt said Mr. Y said Mr. X's defense had no bearing on the plea bargain. However, I feel it needs to be known to you and others in the court system of Mr. X's behavior so no other family has to feel they were underserved when their/our tax dollars pay his salary. I do plan to meet with Matt Dugan and Mr. X to express how I and my grandson felt marginalized by his lack of preparation and defense.*

Thank you for taking the time to read this letter and I again want to express how I appreciate the way you carry out your duties as a judge in what I'm sure can be quite challenging trying to figure who is telling the truth.

May the Lord continue to bless you with wisdom, compassion, and discernment.

To God be the glory,
Sheran R. White

Chapter Seven
THE PARTY

Recently we had a graduation party for Devon's youngest brother, DeonDre, and I said to the oldest grandson, Jerome, "I don't know how you are going to take this. I don't know if I would be as happy about DeonDre's graduation if Devon was still alive and in prison, or at home sick, lying in bed and waiting to die." The commencement party took place on my birthday. I'm 60 years old now, a milestone in life. I thank God that He took care of all that so we could truly celebrate DeonDre's graduation. God impressed upon me that Devon is in a much better place than we will ever be, until we get there. Instead of us having the burden of him still being in prison or laying in a prison bed, at home, or in a hospice, God simply called him home.

On June 30, 2017, that facility on the Northside, SCI-Pittsburgh, where Devon spent his last two years on this side of life, closed its doors for good. That would have been difficult if he was still ill and had been transferred. We would not have known where he ended up until he contacted us. He was so sick that he probably would not have been able to contact us. A lot of other moms and parents didn't know where their children were going until they got that phone call once they had gone through intake at their new home prison. I refer to them as children, because they are and will always be our children.

I thought my sixtieth birthday was going to be gut-wrenching and sad. My previous birthdays had gone uncelebrated for years since both my son and grandson died in March. When my son died in March of 2007, I was turning 50 that June. There was no big celebration for my birthday then and there hasn't been one since. I turned 60 in June in 2017 and my Devon died in the prison in March 2017. I assumed it would be another uncelebrated milestone for me, and I was prepared to let it pass unnoticed. I also didn't want my grandson DeonDre's commencement to be overshadowed by my sixtieth birthday, so I told everyone we couldn't have any type of celebration unless and until we celebrated his event.

To my surprise, my sixtieth was one of my best birthdays ever, one reason being that I hadn't been to a commencement in years. As I reported earlier, Devon got his GED in prison. All the boys fell behind in their academics because it was hard to get them to focus in school due to all the losses. Therefore, DeonDre's was the first commencement for our family in years. It was exciting and invigorating. All the parents were cheering their kids as they came down in the procession. As we cheered our DeonDre, it was of course bittersweet after laying Devon's body to rest just three months earlier.

DeonDre graduated from a charter school called PACS. It's a school for kids who have struggled with the normal setting of high school because they have encountered trauma, dysfunctional homes, or can't seem to focus. I was impressed and moved that all the graduates who got up there expressed their appreciation to the faculty for this milestone. At one point in their lives, school didn't mean anything because of whatever had happened to them. Despite that, they all testified to the fact that PACS really worked with them. These kids were crying, realizing the mistakes they would have made had they not gone on to finish high school, and then go on to college. They realized that there is more to life than what they had been through, and so much more of their lives were ahead of them. The teachers and school gave them hope beyond what they had endured.

J.T. Thomas, the former Steelers defensive back, was the guest speaker and gave a wonderful speech of encouragement and inspiration. I watched every student run over to one teacher, whose name is Mrs. Boyd. She is from Trinidad and still has a strong accent. The love they had for her was overwhelming. I saw her at the end of the commencement and stopped to tell her how moved I was at how highly the kids spoke of her. I thanked her for how much she invested in them, giving them the hope they needed. She asked who was my child and I said DeonDre Marshman. She said, "Ahhh, he is a good boy and has overcome so much." She said she was proud of him.

The day after my birthday was the big graduation party for our DeonDre. I felt as if I was able to celebrate my milestone of turning 60. I invited sixty people, and it was a lot of fun. Our family hadn't had too many things to celebrate for quite some time. We had a life-sized picture of Devon there with his diploma, along with DeonDre's diploma. We had Devon's name on the cake, because he got his diploma in 2015, but there was no celebration because he was in prison. (We had celebrated his life well-lived at his homegoing service just three months earlier.) Many days make me sad when I think about him, and then I must focus on where he is. I beat myself up sometimes that we didn't get a paid lawyer. Maybe the outcome would have been different, but I didn't have any more money after posting the excessive bond to have him released until the trial. I used all my money to bail him out.

I thought of Devon during the graduation. He would have been so proud of DeonDre. He was one of those kids who talked about others, and always wanted to know what everyone else was doing and how they were doing. I told my sister at the party that the last time we visited Devon when he made his decision about not going on with the medication, she was the first person he asked about. That's the kind of kid he was.

Great peace came on me when I realized the commencement was on my birthday, for I knew only God could arrange that. I knew it was God reminding me of where my grandson is, which He constantly does. Whenever I have those moments of sadness, I bring myself into the now and think about where Devon is at this very moment. I told a coworker recently that I woke up after having a dream about all my kids. My son, my daughter, all six of my grandkids (but not my husband) were in this dream with me, and we were in the bedroom of my house. They were all around me and looking out my two bedroom windows at a tornado that was approaching. Then the house started shaking and we could see the swirling wind from the tornado coming past the window. No one was saying anything but me. I warned them to hold on, which they did, and miraculously our house just stayed where it was. Then I woke up. That summarized for me what our family had been through but we are still standing and praising God.

Chapter Eight
AFRICA

I told someone at Grief Share (I'll explain that later) that it's amazing I was in such deep grief in March, knowing God was sending me to Guadalajara, Mexico on a missions trip in July, and I didn't know how I was going to accomplish everything I needed to do. And obviously, it was something He wanted done. After my son was killed, my grandsons died in a fire, and my husband passed, God sent me to Kenya, while I was a broken woman. Today, after my grandson's death, I'm not as broken because I know He will get me through. So how did He get me through? He sent me away again, this time to lead a team to Mexico. Before he sent me as a team member to Kenya, but this time He trusted me to be able to endure the pain but also to be His hands and feet in Mexico.

I thank Pastor John Stanko for his listening to God's small still voice back in 2010 when he approached me in the café at ACAC. I was totally broken, discouraged, and self-medicating on wine. I was overweight and deeply depressed. I was sitting in the café and no one was talking to me, because people were afraid to talk to me. I was sitting there by myself, and I rarely go to the café even to this day. Pastor John Stanko came in, came over to me, and told me he believed the Lord was telling him to invite me to go on a missions trip to Kenya. After praying, I decided to go, but I went kicking and screaming because I felt I had nothing to give and there was nothing there that was going to help me. I was wrong on both counts.

I had my head down, but I looked up at Pastor Stanko and said maybe I would go in three years. I thought that would get him away from me so he would leave me alone. To my shock he replied, "You could be dead in three years!" And I thought, "Well, after all I have been through, I know he's right." Then I gave him a typical response, "I'll pray about it," knowing I wasn't going to pray about anything. After that, I didn't give it another thought and had no intention of going. It didn't mean anything to me.

Ironically, everything from that point seemed to direct my attention to Africa. I'd see something on TV or hear it on the radio. I ran into what appeared to be a whole family from Africa at Giant Eagle on the Northside of Pittsburgh, and that was the final straw. It was at that point that I surrendered to His will for my life and said, "Okay, Lord, I will go." I didn't want to go, and it still didn't make any sense to me. What in the world would I have to offer a Kenyan? I was so overweight I could barely breathe. They certainly weren't going to give me any wine over there. I was so depressed and what would I have to offer? When I said yes and started making the plans, I'm sure I asked Pastor Stanko a million questions and set about the task of raising the money to go. I raised $4,000 in 28 days.

Then I mentioned to Pastor Stanko that I didn't want to do the Christmas office gift exchange and he suggested I do something in line with going to Kenya. He sent me some information from the SARAH Network and one of the widows' groups jumped out at me. It was one of the first times I realized I was a widow too. I knew it, but I never really said it. That's how I got started raising money for the widows over there. I raised $1,200 that first year there, and I raised that in about two months. Out of that was birthed the idea for the Five James Foundation. I didn't realize all of those who died in my family had the name James until one day I was writing all their names down. And I thought, "That would be a good name for the nonprofit I was starting," again at the suggestion of Pastor Stanko.

I don't remember much from the first time I went to Kenya. It was all a blur. I do remember a few pictures Pastor Stanko took of me looking out the window. I cried a lot while I was there, but I can't even remember much of what we did. When we got home, I felt God directing me to go back the next year. He told me to go every year until 2016. When we got there in 2016, at the airport he told me, I wouldn't be going back there in 2017.

When I got back from Kenya in 2016, I felt God was telling me He was going to send me to a Spanish-speaking country. Therefore, I started investigating community college classes where I could learn Spanish. Suddenly, things started coming to me in Spanish for Grief Share and Divorce Care. I told Pastor Glenn Hanna, our missions pastor, and he said he felt the Lord was directing him to ask me to lead a team to Guadalajara. I promised I would pray about it, and as soon as I said I would go, those emails I was receiving in Spanish never came to me again.

When Devon was incarcerated, he took a great interest in the Five James Foundation, the nonprofit organization I founded to honor the memory of our other family members who were gone. I don't think any of them really understood what I was trying to do. Devon always wanted to know where I was going and when I was coming back, what the Five James Foundation was doing, and how it did what we did. It was like he matured in prison, and his conversations started to mature.

I know He was in all of this. How could I not know all of that? I could not have gone to Mexico if my grandson was lying and dying in a hospital bed, or if I did not know where he was imprisoned. I could go to Mexico because I know where he is. I asked Devon in the hospital where he was with his faith. He looked at me and said, "Grandma, you know I took care of that a long time ago." We talked about his faith a lot, and he shared it with many others in prison.

It was because of his request for copies of Pastor Rock's sermons that the sermon copies are still being sent to county, state, and federal prisons. Devon would always share the sermons with fellow inmates. Before the sermons would reach him, they had to be opened and reviewed by a guard, as was all incoming mail for the inmates. So not only were they being read by the inmates but also the guards prior to Devon receiving them. God's plan to get the Gospel inside those walls to give hope to the hopeless was far reaching, so much further than Devon or I had imagined.

I told my daughter I was more certain of where

Devon is than I am of my son, his two little ones who died in the fire, or my husband. Looking back, I can see the hand of God in all of this. Once again, His word doesn't return to Him void and the truth in Jeremiah 29:11 is relevant today: "'For I know the plans I have for you,' declares the Lord, 'plans to prosper you and not to harm you, plans to give you hope and a future.'" Devon's future was already laid out before him, secure in God's presence.

As I reflect on all the deaths, I can see our Lord made sure I knew they were all saved. Before my son was shot, he told me that when we were in Ocean City, Maryland, he had received Christ watching that "Billy Graham dude" one night on TV. On the day before the fire, I had my grandsons overnight and was putting socks on the four-year-old. He was laying on the bed with his feet in the air and he said, "Grandma, I wuv church." Everyone called the ten-year-old "preacher boy." He found salvation through Christ at Pine Valley Camp with DeonDre. When Pine Valley heard about the fire, the leaders sent me a picture of him receiving Christ as his personal Savior with one of the other students. I know where they are, but I know even more firmly that Devon is in the presence of God. That's where my peace comes from – knowing that His plan was much better than my plan. My grandson was ready, and knew where he was going.

Chapter Nine
GRIEF SHARE

While I was still going to Kenya, God impressed upon me to reach out to widows there. One of our pastor contacts there identified five widows in a village by the name of Banana. I raised some money for them to help themselves, and today their work is going strong. It is quite satisfying to know that through the Five James Foundation, a ministry God gave me, I have helped to make a difference in their lives.

The work with Kenyan widows created a desire for me to work for widows here at home. My church did not have a ministry for widows. By chance, I was invited to a Christmas party hosted by my dear friend, Rita. I was seated beside a woman who belonged to Christ Church at Grove Farm. We began talking and she told me her name. Her last name was unique and I mentioned that I went to high school with a guy by that last name. I told her his name and immediately she exclaimed, "He's my husband!"

Once she heard my testimony, she informed me that her church, Christ Church at Grove Farm, had a newly formed ministry to widows. She gave me the contact information and when I went, I was welcomed there with open arms. They had a Christmas retreat and invited me to attend at the Kearns Spirituality Center. I didn't know any of those women, but they treated me as a sister in the faith and made me feel welcome like I was among family. I will always treasure that weekend where I felt the Lord ministering to me where I accepted the reality that I was a widow. I still go there for all their events for widows. It is always a special time being with them. After going there four or five times, I wondered why I had to go all the way out there to a suburban church to find a ministry to widows.

Therefore, I asked my pastor during a staff devotional meeting why we had no outreach to widows in our church. He agreed that we had erred, and he suggested we talk about it, that maybe I could facilitate it. My first thought was, "Not me, I'm a widow myself." The widows' ministry was started and placed under the Adult Life Ministry at my church. As it grew, the women there discovered I had the Five James Foundation. Every time we met, I would give one of the widows in attendance a $150 gift card to Giant Eagle, a local grocery chain. When I did that, the widow would call and ask how I knew they needed some help. Then I got a few men to be a part of the ministry who could help with repairs, plumbing, and roofing, and all kinds of handyman work. When the ladies needed something, they could call those wonderful men and know they could be trusted with a fair fee for service.

Five James Foundation has paid for three women to have their roofs repaired here in Pittsburgh. We have sent kids to summer day camp. Recently we paid the fee for two single-mom families and their children to attend the ACAC summer day camp. Widows come from other churches, but it's not a support group since we don't really talk about our situations. We just have a good time of fellowship, fun, food, and laughter, and that's how it all got started.

Grief Share is a program put together by a Christian couple and is a solid, biblically-based support group that ministers to grieving people. Initially, I didn't think it was something I would be interested in, but I have learned that it's a great tool to help navigate through the journey of grief. It constantly points the participants back to where their help comes from, which is from the Lord. There is no such truth that time heals all wounds. Instead, we are reminded that Jesus heals all wounds. If people don't have Jesus, who is the crutch they need to lean on during these times, they will find something else, like drugs or alcohol. I can tell anyone from personal experience that the best helper is the Lord Jesus Christ. He said He will neither leave nor forsake us, and He won't. It may feel like He has for a while, but He's right there with us.

I have found pleasure in facilitating these sessions. It is a thirteen-week group meeting consisting of a video, workbook, and discussion. God knows me so well and knew the only way I would attend was as a group facilitator because I felt I didn't need that kind of support. I have discovered through these sessions I had things in my heart that needed addressed and managed. Up until I started facilitating, I thought I had dealt with those things. It has been painful but is setting me free from old wounds that would have eventually surfaced, but not in as a healthy way as they do now.

I have learned that it is important to have a group like Grief Share. Most don't attend when their grief is fresh, for it's hard to hear and focus in the early stage of grief. It seems that most people come about six months into their grieving when they recognize they aren't getting any better and need help. Somehow, they learn about Grief Share and show up. I can see myself being involved with Grief Share for many years to come.

Chapter Ten

THE SYSTEM

The state of our judiciary, at least the part that I encountered with my grandson was very disappointing. It is my hope that through my contacts with some people in the judicial system, they will learn to have more compassion on those coming through the system who are quite young, with an unblemished, non-violent past record. Those young people need to be considered candidates for house arrest, public service, or some other means of discipline before a prison sentence.

Most of the time they are guilty of being young, dumb, and vulnerable. My grandson had no record, had never been in trouble, and no one was physically hurt, but he was still given a harsh sentence. There was no violence or weapon involved. This is in no way meant to demean our judicial system but to urge those who have the power to alter someone's life to search their own hearts and seek the best form of justice that is commensurate with the crime.

A little compassion can go a long way with these often confused and misled young men and women. Before they are considered adults at the age of 21, they are capable of making dumb and unfortunate mistakes, especially committing non-violent offenses. It shouldn't have to cost them their entire life by throwing them into the penitentiary or saddling them with a record that could negatively impact the rest of their lives as they seek to find employment.

I have wondered if my grandson knew whether that car was stolen or not, and I want to say that he did. I think the ADA knew that too, and because Devon didn't tell from whom he got the car, he was given a harsh sentence. I do *not* know that for a fact, because we never talked about it. Only Devon knows the truth and he chose not to reveal that information to anyone. Divulging what he knew would have had consequences, and thus he decided to keep it a mystery.

I don't blame the prosecutors, for they were only doing their job. I do fault the public defender, however, who represented us, if that's what it can be labeled. His legal representation was comprised of showing up without so much as a folder with any information on my grandson. As I related earlier, I made my disgust with him known to the sentencing judge, the prosecutors, and head of the public defender office. My prayer is that the legacy of my grandson will give cause for pause in sentencing silly young men whose only real mistakes are that of being misguided and ignorant of the judicial and prison systems until they come face to face with them.

It's not a bad system but it is best if you never find yourself caught up in it. It can be life altering with long-term implications. No one wants to see their loved ones in prison. It not only impacts the life of the accused but the entire family is impacted. This is clearly stated in the Bible in Romans 13:

> Let everyone be subject to the governing author-ities, for there is no authority except that which God has established. The authorities that exist have been established by God. Consequently, whoever rebels against the authority is rebelling against what God has instituted, and those who do so will bring judgment on themselves. For rulers hold no terror for those who do right, but for those who do wrong. Do you want to be free from fear of the one in authority? Then do what is right and you will be commended. For the one in authority is God's servant for your good. But if you do wrong, be afraid, for rulers do not bear the sword for no reason. They are God's servants, agents of wrath to bring punishment on the wrongdoer. Therefore, it is necessary to submit to the authorities, not only because of possible punishment but also as a matter of con-science. This is also why you pay taxes, for the authorities are God's servants, who give their full time to governing. Give to everyone what you owe them: If you owe taxes, pay taxes, if revenue, then revenue; if respect, then respect; if honor, then honor (Romans 13:1-7).

I am not bitter at all. As a matter of fact, I pray for the sentencing judge, the prosecutors, and all those I have encountered within the prison and justice systems. My prayer is that God would give them the ability to discern the truth, have compassion as they handle each case, and find wisdom in their sentencing. My family and I hold nothing against any of them.

As mentioned in a note from the prosecutor, it was a difficult case in which my grandson found himself. The prosecutor stated that he noticed the love I had for my grandson and that Devon handled his difficult case in an upright and dignified manner. When I got that lovely letter from the Assistant District Attorney, I sent him a thank you card like I sent everyone else, thanking him for taking the time to send such an encouraging letter. I said we held nothing against him and that he was kind then and even more kind now. I blessed him and wanted him to know that I was praying for him as he moved people through the system.

My grandson made a choice, and the consequences that came with it had nothing to do with the court system. It's just how it is. When people, black or white, find themselves caught up in that, they never know how it's going to turn out. It's best that they don't ever go there. I hold nothing against the system, for it's the best it can be considering how other countries handle cases. We wouldn't have been there had it not been for Devon making the decision to get behind the wheel.

At the same time, I am not faulting my grandson. He was being the immature, silly boy that had no clear understanding of the consequences that follow when he became an adult at the tender age of 18 and was faced with a reality over which he had absolutely no control. God is the one who has all the power and authority. No matter how things may have appeared and turned out, we still have the victory because my grandson was ushered into the presence of our Lord when he most needed Him.

Our Lord put all the right people within the justice and prison systems in my grandson's life during his last four years of that experience – even that poor excuse of an attorney, the public defender. Because of his poor representation of my grandson, someone reading this may be inclined to look into what is going on in the area of public defense so it doesn't happen to anyone else. I honestly don't know how that public defender sleeps at night.

In the letter from the assistant DA, he told me how to go about clearing my grandson's records, which I can't do until the year 2020. He said if I had any problems or questions to call him for help. Come 2020, I will get his record expunged. Just as I had a strong urging to write this book now, having his record expunged is another thing I feel strongly I need to accomplish.

Life has gone on for our family. Let me close with a report of how we are all doing as of the writing of this book.

Chapter Eleven

TODAY

Our family has always been close and strong, and we are even closer now. We have a group text group comprised of myself; my daughter, Ebony; her two boys, Jerome & DeonDre; my granddaughter, Paje; and daughter-in-law, Aisha. If someone doesn't text us in two or three days, one of us will contact that person. If someone doesn't respond, I take it upon myself to initiate contact. We constantly keep in touch and encourage each other and even talk about the hard times we may be having at that moment.

My daughter is grieving, but she is doing okay. She has reached out to me a couple of times for support and has apologized to me that she really didn't know the pain I was in when her brother, my son, was killed. Now she knows what it feels like when a mother loses a child. She knows now that she probably could have been more supportive, but you only learn that from experience. I'm sorry she has to go through this because it's horrible.

I am writing this because I want people to know who my grandson truly was. He was the second born and like me, people tend to pay little attention to that middle child. No one remembers that child or gets to know them. Everyone knows Jerome the oldest and DeonDre the baby, but Devon was in the middle. I also want people to know that he wasn't a bad kid or a hardened criminal. There is a stigma when someone says that they have a loved one who is imprisoned. People's facial expression changes, whether they realize it or not, as well as their posture.

I watch people react when I tell them that my grandson died in prison. They don't realize they are doing it. They react as if his life was somehow worth less, but it wasn't. He wasn't in there for some violent crime, and in my mind, it did not affect who he was or his worth. My grandson made an impact on his fellow inmates before he got sick and they were all separated and dispersed. That prison on the Northside held a couple thousand young men. I believe God used my grandson to be a light in a very dark place. That thought is confirmed from the letter received from the chaplain of SCI-Pittsburgh that was read at his home-going service. He let his light shine before men that "they may see your good works, and glorify your Father who is in heaven."

I am feeling joyful and happy, realizing I'm no longer in such deep pain. For four years, when I read Devon's emails, I was in so much pain, but few realized it. I was walking around with a heavy burden, dealing with him being sick and in prison, and not being able to be there for him as his grandmother, outside of the few times we were permitted to visit. I'm not in that kind of deep pain anymore. I'm not grieving as I did with the other deaths, and that's not because I loved him any less. It's because I know what I know and what I know is where he is, and that God's plan was much better than my own. I would be in pain right now with my plan, trying to keep him here and care for him. I have truly let that intense pain from his passing go. I still miss him and shed tears, but they aren't tears of hopelessness. As His Word says, "But we do not want you to be uninformed, brethren, about those who are asleep, so that you will not grieve as do the rest who have no hope" (1 Thessalonians 4:13).

It took me longer with the other deaths, and I told Pastor Stanko after my first trip to Kenya that somehow I was able to bury my loved ones, so to speak, while I was in Kenya. I was able by God's grace to dig up the pain and yield it to Him, and He buried it for me. I came home and lost weight. I stopped drinking. I got involved helping others.

I had often watched the ads over here for relief agencies working in drought-ravaged sections of Africa. I saw the pictures of the pitiful children with flies crawling all over their distended stomachs, deformed by malnutrition. I used to ask, "God, where are you in all of that?" Then I went to Africa and saw some of those deprived children and they were happy in the Lord. They prayed, they smiled, and I had the answer to my question: Where was God? He was right there.

That is the answer to my own situation. If you were to ask, "Where was God in all the deaths in your family?", I would answer, "He was right there!" He was there to comfort and heal, and bring good out of tragedy. The correct question is not, "Where are you God?" but rather, "What am I doing to take God to those situations others are experiencing?"

I found a few favorite passages in all this. One is from the Old Testament in Nahum 1:7: "The Lord is good, a refuge in times of trouble. He cares for those who trust in him," and Romans 8:28: "And we know that in all things God works for the good of those who love him, who have been called according to his purpose."

I am amazed that the only two letters I received about Devon's character and faith were from two people who knew him the shortest amount of time; but turns out they knew him the best. They were the Assistant District Attorney, who was the prosecuting attorney in his case, and the chaplain from the prison in which he spent the last years of his life. I believe God used these exceptional people to show how far-reaching our Lord's arms are for those who love Him and are called according to His purpose. Although that period in Devon's and my life were what most would see as dark, God, who is able to do exceedingly abundantly above all we can imagine or think, showed up just as He has for His people throughout the ages.

Someone recently asked me what is the attribute of God that I have seen through all of this, and I responded His faithfulness. He is faithful and has been faithful for the past ten years during this journey through the valley of the shadow of death. The rest of Psalm 23 is also true:

> Even though I walk
> through the darkest valley,
> I will fear no evil,
> for you are with me;
> your rod and your staff,
> they comfort me.

You prepare a table before me
in the presence of my enemies.
You anoint my head with oil;
my cup overflows.
Surely your goodness and love will follow me
all the days of my life,
and I will dwell in the house of the LORD forever.

You can follow the Five James Foundation on Facebook
or contact me at sheranzellouswhite@gmail.com

ACKNOWLEDGMENTS

First, I want to take the time to thank our Lord and Savior, Jesus Christ, for always being who He has said He is, before and during the time I finally accepted Him as Lord over my life. He has been faithful even when I was still a sinner; He died for me (us).

Pastor John Stanko, thank you for your faithfulness and obedience in His "Quest" of using your gifts to help people discern and direct their own "Quest" in life. Thank you for that first encounter in the café at Allegheny Center Alliance Church in 2010 and the bold response, "You could be dead in three years." It was an awakening that brought me to this point of clarity, peace, and trust.

Two ladies who have been with me throughout

this journey are DeVorne Puryear James and Loleda Moman, who know me well enough to ignore me when I say, "No, I'm good." You have been there behind the scenes helping when I was sick physically by preparing meals and going as far as shopping for food and over-the-counter meds for me, and when the load was too heavy for me to carry. Thank you for all your help during those times when I would have dropped the ball with the arrangements of the funerals and the repasts. I never had to ask; you both knew what to do. Like Nike says, "Just Do It" and you just did it.

Thank you to Pastor Wayne and Leeann Younger for all the time you invested in ministering to me when I first got word about the fire. You were there every day for weeks during and afterwards. Leeann, I will never forget how you arrived every day, and sat with me for hours and ministered to me in silence. You both made sure my kids were fed and I was left to my thoughts as you quietly sat there, not expecting anything in return from me. If I never said thank you, I am saying it now.

A special thank you to Ken and Mona Hawkins. You know what you did for my family and me and we haven't forgotten. You have shown how Christmas should be celebrated, sharing and giving with nothing expected in return. That act of kindness and generosity at that time was a blessing and continues to bless me: the gift (blessing) that keeps on giving (blessing). We talk about it every Christmas, and what you did has shaped the way I celebrate Christmas even now. Thank you again for being His hands and feet at that time.

Thanks to Pastors Rock Dillaman and Blaine Workman. Pastor Rock, thank you for the sound biblical teachings over the years that have equipped me with truth thus allowing me to see this journey through God's eyes and not just mine. Pastor Blaine, I appreciate you always listening to me, even when you did not want to as I barged into your office excited about something. But seriously, thank you for the beautiful service for my grandson, Devon Rae Marshman. The time you took to spend with my family and me so you could really get to know Devon was far beyond our expectations. Also, thank you for taking the time with me over the four years leading up to his passing, providing wisdom, prayer, and genuine interest.

Thank you Stephanie Wood, Director of Nursing State Correctional Institute-Pittsburgh, for openly expressing your love for Devon and treating him and the other inmates in the infirmary like human beings and not worthless inmates. Rev. Tami Hooker, Facility Chaplaincy Program Director at the State Correctional Institute-Pittsburgh, thank you for spending time with us and Devon during his last four hours of life here on this side; and apprecation to Assistant District Attorney, Allegheny County Christopher Stone, for the kindness you have shown Devon, my family, and me during one of the most difficult times in our lives. You all were in an awkward position, but able to show compassion without wavering from your appointed duties as public officials. Also, my thanks to the Honorable, Judge Philip Anthony Ignelzi, Court of Common Pleas Allegheny County, for professionalism and compassion in the way you conduct your court proceedings. You always paid attention to the facts that helped you discern who was telling the truth. I will continue to pray for all of you as you move people through the systems of justice and prison.

I also want to thank my hair stylist, Dionna Jackson (bka as Dee) from StudioX Hair Salon. Thank you for always taking such good care of my hair and for the style on the back of this book; also, for the godly environment of worship music when being served.

I can't forget Ann Taylor. Thank you for introducing me to the high-quality, high-fashion clothing and the professional staff with whom I work. The dress and necklace on the back cover are just one of the beautiful items from your line of clothing and jewelry.

Last but not least, thanks to G. Keith and Sally Turnbull. I will always cherish the time when you took me for a long ride in your mobile home at a time when I was so broken; you saw me and took action. You fed and comforted me, not to mention all the other times you blessed my family and me. Thank you from the depths of my heart.

Thank you to all the others who have prayed for us over the years, especially my ACAC family. I love you all so much; there are far too many to mention. Please keep praying for us as we continue to trust God and walk this journey knowing He will never leave us nor forsake us. Your continued prayers are what keep our eyes fixed upon Jesus and not the circumstances we have found ourselves in over the past ten years.

To God be the glory.